N

D ✕   C
       B   ✕ E

✕ G   H ✕

              F

✕ J   I ✕

M

Section F fits
over here

Cut the wooden dowel this wide

A

HOW SCIENCE WORKS

CARS, TRAINS & MOTORBIKES

CHRIS OXLADE

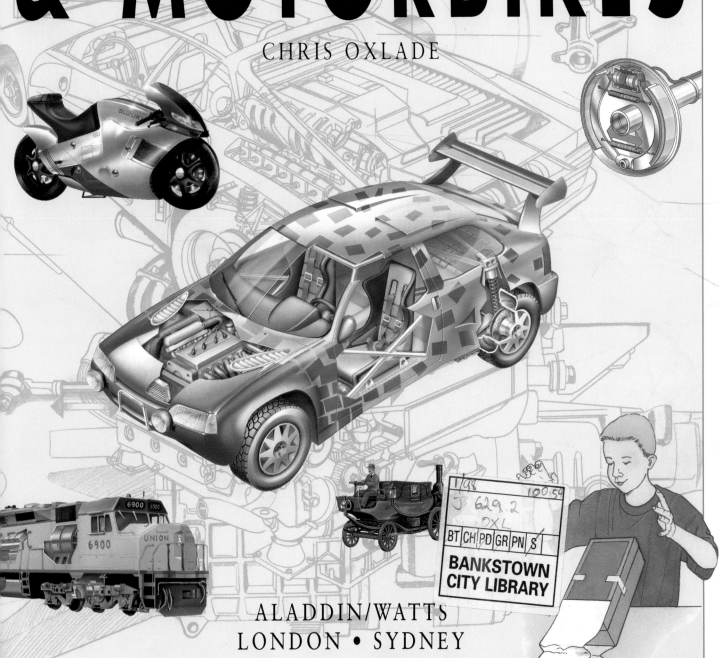

ALADDIN/WATTS
LONDON • SYDNEY

CONTENTS

INTRODUCTION

Land vehicles come in all shapes and sizes, from the biggest train to a scooter that can be packed into the boot of a car. But almost all vehicles have wheels. They all need engines to drive them forward, and they all need brakes to stop.

Look inside cars, trains and motorbikes and discover the science that makes them work. Then test out your knowledge by building a model – just like the designers of a Formula 1 racing car!

To make the projects, you will need: thick and thin card, corrugated card, elastic bands, a craft knife, scissors, PVA glue, strong clear glue, paper clips, acrylic paint, a felt tip pen case, wooden dowel, a bendy drinking straw, a stapler and staples, thin wire and tin foil.

Motor car
project box

Science experiment
project box

© Aladdin Books Ltd 2000

Designed and produced by
Aladdin Books Ltd
28 Percy Street
London W1P 0LD

First published in
Great Britain in 2000 by
Franklin Watts
96 Leonard Street
London EC2A 4XD

ISBN 0 7496 3865 6

A catalogue record for this
book is available from the
British Library.

Printed in Belgium
All rights reserved

Editor
Jim Pipe

Science Consultant
Dr Bryson Gore

Series Design
David West Children's Books

Designer
Simon Morse

Illustrators
Ian Thompson, Catherine Ward,
Simon Tegg, Alex Pang, Gerald
Witcomb, Don Simpson, Aziz
Khan, David Russell, Ron
Hayward, Graham White,
Peter Harper, Ross Watton
and Simon Bishop.

Picture Research
Brooks Krikler Research

THE SCIENCE OF MOTION

Cars, trains and motorbikes are like all moving objects. To get around, they must accelerate (speed up), keep their speed and decelerate (slow down).

They often need to change direction, too. But they will only change speed or direction when a force acts on them. In vehicles, these forces come from the engine, brakes and wheels.

Steam engines were the first form of power for vehicles. This steam car appeared in 1854.

THE FORCES ON A VEHICLE

Several different forces act on a vehicle as it moves along. Thrust is the force created by the engine which pushes the vehicle forward. It works by the tyres gripping the road's surface.

Two forces act in the opposite direction. They are drag, created by the air flowing past when the vehicle is moving, and friction, which tries to stop the car's moving parts sliding against each other.

Thrust created by the engine drives the vehicle forward.

CONTROLS

Electronic systems make vehicles safer and cheaper. They include anti-lock braking, engine management and navigation systems (see page 20 to find out more).

Because of gravity's pull, more power is needed to go uphill than downhill. Gravity also presses the tyres onto the road.

BODY AND STRUCTURE

A vehicle needs a solid structure to support its heavy mechanical parts. A strong body also helps to protect passengers from injury (*right*).

Drag slows down a moving vehicle.

Friction in the wheel bearings slows down a vehicle. See page 6 to find out why.

Gravity pulls the vehicle downward.

ENGINES AND MOTORS

Most vehicles have petrol engines, where the fuel burns inside cylinders. The engine releases the energy stored in the fuel and uses it to make the car move along. Electric trains and some cars have electric motors instead of petrol engines (see page 19).

WHEELS

Wheels let a vehicle roll smoothly along. Their tyres create friction with the road, causing traction (grip) for acceleration and for braking (*above*). Some trains are held clear of their tracks with magnets (*left*). This removes all friction with the rails (see page 7).

CHAPTER 1 – WHEELS

Friction is a very important for vehicle designers. It's a force that tries to stop surfaces moving against each other. Vehicles without wheels would be useless because the friction between them and the ground would be huge, making them very difficult to move.

WHAT IS FRICTION?

Friction happens between two surfaces because bumps and hollows in the surfaces catch against each other. Even smooth surfaces look quite rough under a microscope (*above*).

 When slippery liquids, called lubricants, are put between the two surfaces, they separate them slightly. This stops the bumps catching and reduces the friction. Moving parts in vehicles are usually lubricated with oil.

Another way of reducing friction is to put balls or cylinders between the surfaces. Only a small part of each ball touches the surfaces at one time, and this reduces friction.

AXLES AND BEARINGS

Wheels are fixed firmly to a vehicle with an axle or a shaft. These help the wheels to turn freely because they are much thinner than a wheel – so there is a smaller surface to create friction.

The axle is supported inside a ring by balls. These reduce friction because they touch only a small part of the axle's surface.

Ball bearing

WHY WHEELS WORK

Wheels reduce friction because they roll with the movement of the vehicle, without any surfaces rubbing together. At the same time they provide grip because of the friction between the tyre and the road.

Maglev (short for magnetic levitation) trains are pushed clear of their tracks by magnets, which reduces the friction to zero.

Magnets

Magnets

TRAIN WHEELS

A train wheel is a solid steel disc. Wheels come in pairs on steel rods called axles. The axles are attached to the train with bearings. Each wheel has a lip (or flange) on the inside rim to stop it slipping sideways off its rail.

Flange

MODEL CAR
PART 1
WHEELS

Add a rubber band to make tyres

4 Roll up a piece of card so that it fits around the dowel, then glue it (*below*). Thread the dowel through and glue the other front wheel to it.

1 To make your car, start with the wheels. Trace eight part **A**s from the plans at the end of the book. Then cut them out from corrugated card.

3 Cut a piece of dowel so that it is just wider than part **M** (see ends). Then glue a front wheel to one end.

2 Glue two part **A**s together to make a front wheel. To make a back wheel, straighten out one half of a paper clip and poke this through a part **A**. Then glue another part **A** to it (*right*). Make two back wheels and two front wheels in all.

Dowel fits in here

A

A

A

SUSPENSION AND TYRES

If a vehicle's wheels were attached firmly to its body, the passengers would feel every bump that the vehicle went over. A suspension system allows the wheels to move up and down under the body, reducing the effect of the bumps.

With a simple spring suspension, the vehicle would keep bouncing after going over a bump. A device called a damper prevents this.

To feel how a spring works, hop up then land without bending your knees. Can you feel the force? That's why you normally bend your knees, because they act like springs to give you a soft landing.

3 Oil stops spring bouncing back.

Make your own springs

Leaf spring

SPRINGS

When a spring is squashed, it stores energy, then releases it when it bounces back. Some springs are coils, others are made of curved plates of metal (called leaf springs). These work like a diving board, but bend in the middle.

A spring also bounces back if it is stretched.

A spring shape will only work if it is made from an "elastic material" – one that returns to its original shape after being squashed or stretched.

AIR SUSPENSION

Some vehicles use air suspension. Instead of metal springs, air is squashed and expands inside a sealed cylinder.

Air

2 After landing the spring is squashed.

1 Before landing, the spring is in its original shape.

MODEL CAR

PART 2

SUSPENSION

1 To make a spring, coil some thin wire around a pen four times (*left*). Then make five more springs like this one.

2 Cut out part **B** from thick card, including the hole for the steering wheel (marked **C**). After this, stick two springs at positions **D** and **E**. Then glue **B** to the front axle section you made on page 7.

3 Cut out part **F** from thick card and stick the other four springs onto it at positions **G**, **H**, **I** and **J**, using strong glue.

DAMPERS

A damper is a cylinder filled with thick oil that surrounds a piston connected to the wheel. After a spring is squashed going over a bump, the thick oil slows down the piston and stops the spring from bouncing back.

TYRES

A modern tyre is made up of many layers. Inside is a tube filled with air that acts like a spring. The outside of the tyre normally has a pattern of grooves. In wet weather, these stop the vehicle from slipping by letting water escape from between the tyre and the road.

Wet weather tyres

Racing cars use tyres with no tread (slicks) in dry weather.

Rubber tread

Rayon

Steel band

Wire

CHAPTER 2 – STRUCTURE

A car's body creates a space for the passengers and their luggage or cargo, and normally supports all the other parts of the car. The body needs to be a strong structure that protects the passengers, and is rigid enough to support the weight of the engine.

It must also be as light as possible to let the car speed up quickly.

You can test how a car's crumple zone works. See the experiment on page 11.

Chassis

Until the 1940s, most cars had a heavy metal chassis that supported the wheels and engine. The body, called coachwork, was built on top. This was often made from wood.

MODEL CAR
PART 3
THE BODY

1 Cut out the body (part **K**) from thin card – and don't forget to cut out the hole for the steering (**L**). Then glue the body together using the tabs.

L

K

M

N

2 Then cut out the base (part **M**) from thick card. At the same time, cut out the hole for the steering (**N**). You have now made the main sections – turn to page 17 to add the power!

MOTORBIKES AND TRAINS

A motorbike frame is made of metal tubes welded together to create a strong but light structure that supports all the other parts of the bike.

Trains are built more like old cars, with the body and engine sitting on a heavy chassis.

Exhaust
Engine
Radiator
Frame

Monocoque structure

BODY SHELLS

Most cars are built around a single-piece metal shell called a monocoque. This is made from sheets of metal pressed into shape and welded together. Other body panels are connected to the shell by bolts and hinges.

Crumple Zones

Crumple zones are sections of a car's body that collapse in a collision, reducing the force of the impact. To see how they work, try this experiment.

1 Find a rectangular box. At one end, tape a sheet of paper (or two) on to make a tube. This makes a rigid crumple zone.

Add a shoe for extra weight

2 Drop the box onto a hard surface on the solid end and it bounces after the hard impact. Now drop the box on its crumple zone and the impact is absorbed as the tube crumples up.

The easier the air can flow around a vehicle, th smaller the drag on the vehicle. A car with good streamlining will go faste and use less fuel than a badly designed one.

STREAMLINING

Drag is the force that tries to slow a vehicle as it moves through the air. The faster the vehicle goes, the bigger drag gets. In fact, if the speed doubles, the drag becomes four times bigger.

Eventually, drag gets as big as the thrust from the engine, stopping the vehicle going any faster.

Streamlining is shaping the vehicle's body to reduce drag.

You can use a model car to test streamlining and drag for yourself.

SMOOTH TRAINS

Streamlining is important for all vehicles. High-speed express trains need careful streamlining at the front. Curved shapes allow the air in front of the train to flow smoothly over, under and round.

High-Speed Cars

City cars hardly ever reach high speeds, so streamlining is less important than it is for cars designed for high-speed motorway travel. Racing cars also have aerofoils, parts that are shaped like a plane's wing. They push the car down, increasing its grip on the road.

Formula 1 car

Aerofoil   Aerofoil

A racing bike has smooth body panels for extra speed.

The smooth shape of these modern town cars helps them to use less fuel.

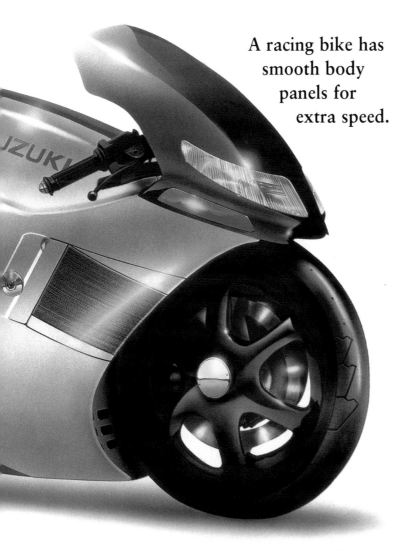

otorbikes have a ooth front section lled a fairing. This ides the air around e motorbike. The er can duck behind o reduce drag, too.

Streamlining

Try this experiment to test out streamlining.

1 Take an old toy car and drop it down the sloping end of a full bath (*bottom*). Place a coin on the bottom of the bath to mark how far it goes.

2 Then find a small, rectangular cardboard box that covers the outside of the car. Tape it over the car, then try sliding the car down the bath again. It won't go as far, because its shape is less streamlined.

BUILDING CARS

Most cars are built on automated production lines in huge factories. As each car body moves along the production line, workers and robots add parts, such as seats and doors. Engines are built on their own production lines before being fitted.

In some car plants, robot vehicles deliver parts to the production line from the parts warehouse.

The car body is made from sheets of steel formed into shape by huge presses and welded together by robot welders.

The first cars produced on a production line were made in the early 1920s by Henry Ford. They were a lot cheaper than cars built one by one.

DESIGN

The look of a new car is worked out by a car designer. The thousands of parts are then designed on a computer.

Before the car is put on the road, models and prototypes are tested for looks, safety and reliability.

Completed cars go through quality control, where they are tested to make sure everything is working properly.

CRASH TESTS

Crash tests demonstrate how well a new car model stands up to different sorts of crashes, such as front and side impacts. Crash-test dummies in the car contain sensors that measure the forces that passengers would feel in the crash.

The body and other panels are painted in an enclosed paint area. Many layers of paint protect the metal against rust.

The engine and gear box are assembled and attached to the body. Then carpets are laid on the floors and the seats are bolted to the floors.

RECYCLING

Cars do not last forever. Many parts, such as break pads and exhaust pipes, wear out after a few years and are replaced.

Eventually, the body begins to rust and lose strength, and then the car is scrapped. Many metal and plastic parts (in green, *below*) can be recycled into new materials to make new cars.

Robots do a lot of the work in a modern factory. But humans are still very important in checking that the work has been done correctly.

CHAPTER 3 – ENGINES

The main picture shows how a single cylinder works. But most engines have from two to eight cylinders.

A vehicle's engine provides the energy needed to move the vehicle along. The job of the engine is to convert the chemical energy stored in fuel into energy that makes the vehicle move.

It does this by burning fuel. This turns chemical energy into heat energy. The heat energy makes the burning gases expand inside a cylinder. The gases push against a piston, which turns the crankshaft.

Camshaft

Valves

Exhaust out

Spark plug

Piston

Crankshaft

Power from Chemicals

In an engine, the pistons are moved by hot gases. These are created during a chemical reaction between fuel and air. In this experiment, gas released from chemicals is used to force your hands apart.

1 Pour four teaspoons of baking soda into an empty plastic drinks bottle and fold the bottle tightly in half.

2 Pour a few teaspoons of vinegar into the bottle and put the top on. Squeeze the bottle between your hands and shake it to mix the chemicals. The reaction creates gas that fills the bottle, forcing your hands apart (*top*).

The crankshaft is linked to the camshaft by a chain or belt. As it turns, the camshaft opens the valves that let fuel and air get into the pistons and exhaust gases get out.

INSIDE A PETROL ENGINE

In a petrol engine, fuel mixed with air burns inside the cylinders. The fuel burns in short bursts, making explosions that create hot gases. The gases push the pistons. These are linked to the gear box by the crankshaft. Waste gases are pushed out of the car through the exhaust system.

The mix of fuel and air is lit by a tiny spark from a spark plug (*left*) powered by electricity.

Carburettor

Air in

Pipe from fuel tank

Fuel in

FUEL AND AIR MIX

Fuel cannot burn without oxygen from the air. So it is mixed with air inside the carburettor before being sucked into the pistons.

MODEL CAR
PART 4
ENGINE

ADULT HELP NEEDED

1 Find a felt tip pen case and cut the top and bottom off it so it is just wider than the rear wheel section (part **F**).

2 After this, ask an adult to cut a section 1 cm wide in the middle of the pen case. Then thread a thick rubber band through the case. Using a strong glue, stick the case along the dotted lines on **F**.

F

3 Take the back wheels you made on page 7 and thread the end of the paper clip on each wheel through a bead (*below*). Then hook the paper clip ends around the end of the elastic band.

paper clips

bead

elastic band

F

4 After adding both wheels, pull the elastic band through the hole in the middle of the pen case. Keep pulling until the band is quite tight and both beads are against the ends of the pen case, but aren't *too* tight (*left*). Then staple the band firmly to **F**.

F

5 Finally, use a strong glue to fix the springs on **F** to part **M**.

M

OTHER ENGINES

Most cars are powered by a petrol engines. But other types of engine are increasingly common. Diesel engines are used in most trucks, and electric motors are used in many trains.

Some engines are also designed to use unusual fuels, such as methane or hydrogen. A few high-speed record-breaking cars have used jet engines.

You can feel how the air and fuel inside a diesel engine heat up as they are squashed.

Hold a finger over the hole in a bicycle pump and push in the handle.

Petrol engine

1 AIR SUCKED IN

Air in →

Piston down

2 PISTON SQUASHES AIR

Piston up

3 FUEL IS LIT

Fuel in

Piston down

4 WASTE GASES OUT

Gases out

Piston up

Crankshaft

THE DIESEL ENGINE

In a diesel engine, air inside the cylinders is squashed (compressed) by the pistons. This makes the air very hot.

Fuel is injected into the air, which is so hot that the thick diesel fuel explodes. This pushes the pistons down and drives the crankshaft around.

ELECTRIC MOTORS

An electric motor turns electrical energy into movement (kinetic energy). Inside the motor, a coil of wire, called a rotor, has magnets around it. When electricity flows through the rotor, the magnets make it spin.

In cars, the electrical energy comes from batteries, where it is stored as chemical energy. But most electric cars can travel only 100 km before their batteries need charging again.

Magnet

Magnet   Rotor   Electricity
supply

HYBRID CARS

Some cars have petrol engines *and* electric motors on each wheel. Batteries provide the electricity for the motors on short journeys.

On long journeys, where the batteries would run down, the engine drives a generator which produces electricity for the motors.

Electric motor

Electric locomotives get power from overhead electric cables, a third electric rail on the track, or a generator driven by a diesel engine.

Electric
cables

ELECTRIC MOTOR

Electricity
supply

Rotor

Magnet

Battery

Motors

19

CHAPTER 4 – CONTROLS

A driver uses simple controls (accelerator, clutch and brake pedals, a gear stick and a steering wheel) to make a car speed up, slow down, and turn.

Many modern cars have complex electronic circuits that help the driver to drive safely and in comfort.

Modern cars have a computer that makes the most efficient use of fuel at different speeds and controls the car's braking and balance.

Navigation

Stabilising controls

Computer

Fuel injection

Anti-Lock Brakes

Add steering to your model.

TODAY'S CAR

We are just entering a new age where we have huge control over our car. In the first cars, levers and springs were used to apply controls. The latest cars combine computers and hydraulics.

Modern cars are also increasingly "green". Filters such as CATs (catalytic convertors) cut out harmful gases that pollute the atmosphere.

If a car stops violently, a bags inflate quickly to sto passengers from going through the windscreen.

air-conditioning systems keep the air inside the car at a comfortable temperature and humidity.

THE BEST ROUTE

In-car navigation systems guide drivers automatically to their destinations. They use a satellite navigation system to work out where the car is, and a database of roads to work out the best route. Some systems can also receive information about traffic jams and navigate around them.

NOT TOO CLOSE!

A few cars have a detection system that warns drivers if they are too close to the car in front, and applies the brakes to stop the car getting any closer.

A similar system warns the driver about objects in the way when the car is reversing.

Power steering

Exhaust system

MODEL CAR
PART 5
STEERING

1 Push a bendy drinking straw through the holes in **M** and **B** and glue it to **B**. Cut out **O**, and glue this to the straw above **M** so that the springs on the front axle touch **M**, but **B** can still turn freely.

Drinking straw

Front wheel section

K

M

2 Now glue **K** to **M**. The straw should poke out of the top of **K**. Try the straw in different slots to steer the car.

GEAR SYSTEMS

A car's transmission system carries the power from the engine to the wheels. It is made up of a gearbox (and normally a clutch) and drive shafts. The faster the engine turns, the more power it produces. Gears allow the engine to turn quickly whether the car is just starting off or speeding along.

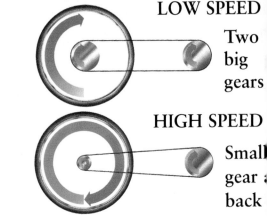

LOW SPEED Two big gears

HIGH SPEED Small gear at back

Two gears the same size spin at the same speed. But if one gear is twice as big as the other, the small gear will spin twice as fast.

Gear stick

Gear wheels

Crankshaft from engine

GEAR BOX

The crankshaft leads to the gearbox, where its speed is reduced by the gear wheels. The gear stick selects a set of gears which make the correct reduction for the car's speed. First gear makes the wheels turn very slowly for starting off. Higher gears make the wheels turn more quickly for driving. The clutch releases the gears from the engine. This allows a smooth change from one gear to another.

The Differential

The differential allows a pair of wheels being driven by the engine to turn at different speeds as a car turns a corner.

When a car drives straight the small differential gears are carried around by the crown wheel. When a car corners, the differential gears spin the two drive shafts at different speeds.

Differential gearwheel

Drive shaft to wheel

Crown wheel

Drive shaft from gear box

Differential gearwheel

Drive shaft to wheel

When a car goes round a tight corner, the wheels on the outside of the corner have to travel further than those on the inside.

Spur gears

Types of Gears

Gear mechanisms are used to transfer power, normally from one spinning shaft to another. They can change the speed and direction of the rotation.

Spur gears are used when the shafts are parallel with each other. Bevel gears connect shafts at right angles. Rack and pinion gears connect a shaft with a straight surface that moves from side to side.

Bevel gears

Rack and pinion gears

CHANGING SPEED AND DIRECTION

To accelerate, a vehicle needs more thrust. This is achieved by sending more fuel to the engine. To slow down, it needs more friction. This is achieved by using the brakes to increase the friction on the wheels. To steer around a bend, a vehicle needs a force acting on it towards the bend. In a car, this force comes from the friction of tyres pushing sideways against the road.

Slide a ruler between your thumb and finger (*above right*). The tighter you grip the ruler, the greater the friction. This is how brakes work.

BRAKES

Brakes work by pressing pads against parts of the wheels. This creates friction that slows the wheels. But if the driver presses too hard on the brake pedal, especially on wet roads, the brakes "lock", making the wheels skid (*above*). An anti-lock braking system (ABS) detects if the wheels are about to skid and releases the brakes slightly.

In drum brakes, each wheel has a drum attached and brake pads press on its inside.

— Drum

In disc brakes, each wheel has a metal disc attached and brake pads press on each side of it.

Brake disc

ROUND THE BEND

Because trains run on tracks, the driver does not need to steer. The force to make the train go round a bend comes from the track pushing sideways on the wheels. If a train corners too quickly, this force would tip it over. Tilting the train (or the track) helps to prevent this from happening.

Motorcyclists lean over as they turn corners. This stops the sideways force on the tyres flipping the bike sideways.

The spinning wheels create a force at right angles to the bike.

Gravity pulls downward

Spin Power

The gyroscopic effect of spinning wheels helps motorbikes and bicycles stay upright when they are moving. The same effect stops a spinning top toppling. Try making a top from a short pencil and circle of card.

Forces at right angles to the spin

Racing car steering system

CAR STEERING

A normal car steering system uses a gear system called a rack and pinion to change the turning motion of the steering wheel into a sideways movement that twists the wheels from side to side. Turn to page 23 to see the special gears used for this.

IN A COLLISION

Any moving object keeps on moving at the same speed unless something stops it or slow it down. This is what we call momentum.

If a car comes to a sudden stop, the drive and passengers carry on moving because of this momentum. Seat belts help to stop them from being thrown toward the front of the ca

KEEPING SAFE

A huge amount of research goes into making vehicles safer to travel in. Vehicles have two types of safety systems – systems that help to avoid accidents happening in the first place, and systems that protect passengers if an accident does happen.

Emergency telephone

This new-style motorcycle has a lightweight, weatherproof body that protects the driver from wind and rain. The body is streamlined to reduce drag.

SIGNAL FOR SAFETY

Preventing collisions is especially important on the railways, where a single train can carry hundreds of passengers. Complex electronic circuits operate signals and switches. Automatic train protection systems on the trains themselv apply the brakes if the driver goes past a red lig

MODEL CAR
PART 6
PAINTING

1 Finish your car by painting it and adding pieces of silver foil for the headlights.

2 To drive the car, wind up the elastic band by rolling the car backwards along the floor.

The latest display systems project signs onto the inside of the windscreen, where the driver can read them without looking away from the road.

On motorways, electronic signs warn of queues or fog. Signs are designed so they can be read quickly at speed.

50**

Mobile road repairs

Sensors keep cars at a safe distance.

Underground sensors on road

Tunnel for wildlife

NO HANDS!
In the future, cars might be able to drive themselves. Satellites will guide the cars and computers will keep them a safe distance apart.

DIFFICULT DRIVING
Bad weather, such as heavy rain, can make driving dangerous. Windscreen wipers give the driver a better view and temperature sensors warn drivers that ice is likely to form on the road.

SCIENCE PRINCIPLES
LOOK BACK AND TEST YOUR KNOWLEDG

SPEED AND ACCELERATION

Speed is the distance an object covers in a certain time, and is normally measured in metres per second or kilometres per hour. Acceleration is a measure of how quickly an object's speed is changing.

The word "acceleration" is normally used for speeding up, but slowing down is also acceleration (called deceleration), but in the direction opposite to motion.

 (1) *Which vehicle do you think normally accelerates faster, a car or a motorbike?*

FORCE AND POWER

A force is a push or a pull. It has size and direction. Forces can cancel each other out. For example, in a car, thrust pushing forwards can be equal to drag pushing backwards. In science, power is different to force – it is the rate at which an engine produces energy.

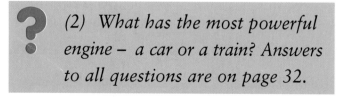 (2) *What has the most powerful engine – a car or a train? Answers to all questions are on page 32.*

DRAG AND FRICTION

Drag and friction are both forces. Drag a force that acts on an object when the object is moving through a fluid (a liqui or a gas), in the opposite direction to th movement. Friction is a force between two surfaces in contact with each other which tries to stop the surfaces rubbing. The bigger the force pressing the surfaces together, the bigger the friction.

(3) *Can you remember why a ball bearing reduces friction? (Turn to page 6 for help).*

HEAT ENERGY

Most energy can be turned easily into a different type of energy. Combustion, or burning, is when the chemical energy in fuel is turned into heat energy.

Heat is also often "waste energy". Have you ever noticed how hot light bulbs get? This is because most of the energy from a candle or a light bulb is turned to heat.

KINETIC ENERGY

Energy comes in two main forms. Potential energy (PE) is stored energy. Kinetic energy (KE) is the energy an object has because it is moving. On a swing, you are constantly changing between having KE and PE.

At the bottom of the swing, you are moving fastest, so your KE is at its greatest. By the time you swing up on the other side, your KE is zero, but your PE is at a maximum because of gravity. If it weren't for drag and friction, you'd swing forever.

KE = 0
PE = Maximum

KE = 0
PE = Maximum

KE = Maximum   PE = Minimum

? *(4) Do you think the energy in fuel is a sort of kinetic energy or a sort of potential energy?*

ELASTICITY

Most materials are elastic, if only a little bit. This means they will return to the same shape again after they have been bent or pulled by an outside force.

Metals are elastic, but they can be made to have more stretch by bending them into a spring.

TECHNICAL TERMS

Chassis — the supporting framework for the body, engine and suspension in older cars.

Compression — decreasing the size of a gas, liquid or solid, normally done by squashing them.

Corrosion — a chemical reaction between a metal, air and water that gradually weakens the metal. Rusting is the corrosion of steel.

Expansion — an increase in size of a gas, liquid or solid, normally because it is heated.

Generator — a device that creates electricity when its central core is spun round. It turns kinetic energy into electrical energy.

Lubricant — any substance that reduces the friction between two surfaces, such as oil or grease.

Recharging — putting electricity into a battery so that the battery can be used again after it has run down.

Sensors — devices that send information to a control system. In a car, sensors might measure the fuel level in the fuel tank or the pressure of the lubricating oil in the engine.

Slicks — Tyres with no tread.

Transmission — A system of shafts and gear boxes that transmits power from the engine to the axles.

Welding — to stick two pieces of metal together using melted metal.

VEHICLE PARTS

Cars and motorbikes may look different to one another, but they often have the same basic parts. Occasionally, new parts are invented, but constant developments make cars cheaper to make and more efficient to run.

1 ENGINE
The engine burns fuel to provide the thrust that moves a car forward.

2 CYLINDERS
Inside the engine are cylinders where the fuel burns. Most car engines have four cylinders.

3 PISTONS
Pistons move up and down inside the cylinders as the fuel burns. They turn a crankshaft which leads to the gearbox.

4 CLUTCH
A clutch disconnects the engine from the gear box while the gears are changed.

5 GEAR BOX
Gears, contained in the gear box, allow the wheel to turn at different speed while maintaining the sam engine speed.

6 DIFFERENTIAL
The differential is a arrangement of gears that allows the driving wheels to turn at different speeds as the ca goes round a corner.

7 DRIVE SHAFT
The drive shaft carries power from the gearbox to the wheels.

CAR SHAPES
A-D show some different car and motorbike shapes. Which do you think are the most streamlined? Answers on page 32.

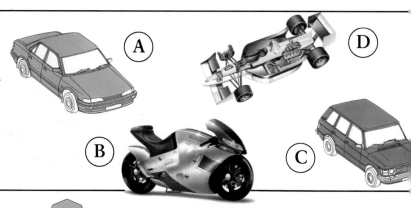

RADIATOR

Water is pumped through pipes inside the engine, cooling it down. The water gets hot and is cooled in the radiator.

SUSPENSION

A system of springs that allows a car's wheels to move up and down over bumps in the road.

TYRES

Most car tyres are designed to grip the road in normal conditions. But special tyres are made for racing cars or rally cars. Can you work out what tyres **A-D**, shown here, are designed for?

0 TYRES

Tyres hold the road surface, providing traction and grip for braking.

1 BRAKES

Brakes create friction to slow a car. A hand brake stops the car rolling when it is parked.

2 FUEL TANK

Where petrol is stored.

13 EXHAUST SYSTEM

Waste gases formed by burning fuel in the engine are carried away into the air by the exhaust system.

14 BATTERY

The battery provides electricity for the motor that starts the engine, and for the lights and other electrical equipment when the engine is switched off.

15 DIESEL ENGINE

Some trains have powerful diesel engines to turn the electrical generators.

16 GENERATORS

When the generators are turned by the diesel engines, they produce electricity. This electricity powers the electric motors.

17 POWERED AXLE

Each axle has electric motors that turn it.

INDEX

The finished model car

Answers: Pages 28–29
1 A motorbike usually accelerates faster than a car because it has a more powerful engine compared to its weight. **2** A train is more powerful than a car because it has to pull a heavier load.
3 Ball bearings reduce friction because they prevent surfaces from sliding against each other.
4 Fuel is chemical energy, which is a form of potential (stored) energy.
Page 30 B & D are the most streamlined shapes.

Page 31 Tyre A is a slick – it is used for racing in dry weather. Tyre B is has a thick tread, designed for off-road racing, Tyre C has a normal tread, used in wet and dry conditions. Tyre D has chains attached to it, for use in snowy conditions.

PHOTO CREDITS
Abbreviations – t – top, m – middle, b – bottom, r – right, l – left, c – centre:
Pages 3, 13 both, 21 & 24-25 – Solution Pictures; 4, 14m, 20b & 24 – Mercedes Benz; 5t, 15t & br & 26 – BMW; 5b & 27 Frank Spooner Pictures; 14tl, m & bl – Ford UK; 20t – Volkswagen.